Celtic motifs

Text and drawings by David Balade

Gill & Macmillan

My sincerest thanks to:

... Michelle de la Rompardais, Don Bernardo, Anh Huan, my forebears, and all who have helped me in my quest.

David BALADE

Published in Ireland 2007 by
Gill & Macmillan Ltd
Hume Avenue, Park West, Dublin 12
With associated companies
throughout the world
www.gillmacmillan.ie

978 0717142224

First published in Great Britain 2007 by
Search Press Limited,
Wellwood, North Farm Road,
Tunbridge Wells, Kent TN2 3DR

Originally published in France 2003 by
Éditions Ouest-France – Édilarge
S.A., Rennes

Publisher's code: 4529 06 05 01 06
Dépôt légal: April 2003 – Printed in France

Copyright © Éditions Ouest-France 2003

English translation by Ian West in association
with First Edition Translations Ltd,
Cambridge, UK

English translation copyright
© Search Press Limited 2007

English edition typeset by GreenGate
Publishing Services, Tonbridge, Kent
Printed by Mame Imprimeurs, 49 Boulevard
de Preuilly, 37000 Tours, France

Ouest-France wishes to thank the Conseil
Général du Morbihan for the generous loan
of the photo (D. Truffaut) of Stone 19 from
the Gavrinis Cairn (56).

Photography credits:

Introduction
Page 4 © Musée d'Angoulême: the Agris
Helmet. Photo: Gérard Martron
Page 5 © Conseil Général du Morbihan:
Stone 19 from the Gavrinis Cairn.
Photo D. Truffaut
Page 6 © Musée de Bretagne, Rennes: detail
of Jacques Philippe sideboard; detail of
woman's bodice in Bigouden style
Page 9 © Musée national du Moyen Age,
Paris: Boatmen's Pillar (Roman Baths, Hôtel
de Cluny). Photo RMN, Gérard Blot

Chapter photographs
Page 10 © Mer et Mer Valéry Hache: Wave.
Page 28 © Michel Coz: Low Tide at La
Trinité-sur-Mer.
Page 46 © Yvon Boëlle: Huelgoat Forest
Page 64 © Bruno Roux: Kercadoret
Page 80 © Jon Arnold Images/Alamy:
Celtic Cross

Editing: Catherine Dandres-Franck

Design and layout: Polymago – Isabelle
Chêne, Pierre-Julien Descoins.

The majority of the motifs in this book are
by David Balade.

Contents

Introduction

The triskele, knotwork, spirals, the tree of life ... all familiar to students of Celtic and Breton motifs. But Celtic art also encompasses the exquisite pages of the Book of Kells, the exuberant plasticity of the **Agris Helmet** discovered in Charente and the stunning abstract mirror from Desborough in England. Celtic art forms have recurred throughout history and are now instantly recognisable, popping up on CD inserts, in the logos of Celtic groups, on every type of tourist souvenir, and so on; but these sinuous, organic forms and knots — often extremely complex — are not exclusive to Celtic art. Knotwork, for instance, appears in the frescoes of Ancient Egypt, to be copied several thousand of years later by Coptic and Byzantine artists. Similarly, once a wall decoration in Babylon, the tree of life travelled down the centuries to grace one of the first great Islamic mosques at Damascus. As for the spiral, it was employed by Neolithic Man in his first artistic efforts, while ceramics unearthed the world over show its prevalence among primitive motifs. Closer to home, at least geographically, are the megalithic remains from the Atlantic coast, such as the **Gavrinis** passage graves of the Morbihan region and those at Newgrange in Ireland, which are among the first structures to exhibit this particular decoration.

All these forms were adopted by craftsmen of the Bronze Age and applied to armour, jewellery and artefacts. What makes Celtic art unique is the skill with which artists and artisans combined their motifs — triskele, knotwork, spirals, scrolls and other forms of the tree of life — to cover the entire surface of a helmet, a brooch or the page of a written manuscript, in a way that is highly structured, almost obsessive. Thus, from the earliest tentative efforts in the 9th to 7th centuries BC up to the Viking invasions (c. AD 1000), Celtic artists exploited every permutation of these motifs for both symbolic and

Stone 19 from the Gavrinis Cairn. Photo: D. Truffaut. Property of the Conseil général du Morbihan.

The Agris Helmet, Celtic artefact from the 4th century BC. Property of the French state. Musée des Beaux-Arts d'Angoulême. Photo: Gérard Martron.

decorative purposes. Contrary to the views of the Greeks and Romans who came into contact with ancient Celtic culture, or, in later times, the detractors of medieval art, Celtic art is in reality bound by a logic and a set of rules all its own, with an aesthetic developed over hundreds of years. Celtic art made its appearance in the 8th century BC in Central Europe (Austria, southern Germany, eastern France) with what is known as the **Halstatt Style**. This period corresponds to the dawn of the Iron Age in Europe when craftsmen began to use the new material to create primarily — at least according to archaeological evidence — figures of animals (cows and bulls but particularly birds), cooking pots and wine seals, incorporating motifs such as stylised *rouelles* (spoked wheels) and hero figures. The most outstanding among other grave goods are magnificent chariots and the earliest torques, heavy necklaces popular throughout the history of Celtic art. At this time northern Europe was to some extent still under the aesthetic influence of the dominant Mediterranean civilisations: Greek, Etruscan, Phoenician. From the 5th century BC the Celts began to leave their homelands in central Europe and emigrate further west to present-day Spain and east to Turkey. Paradoxically, this period, known as **La Tène**, is characterised by the assertion of Celtic art over its Mediterranean models. The Celtic genius was beginning to blossom. The friezes of the classical world — lyres, palmettes and peltas — were beginning to deconstruct and reform into early examples of triskeles, knotwork and new, freer organic forms. At the same time, Celtic art distanced itself from representation of the real world to produce designs ever more abstract and indisputably symbolic. The La Tène period ended with the Roman invasion of Celtic territory in around 50 BC.

The art of the **Gallo-Roman** period attempted the difficult union of Celtic imaginary art forms with the more structured representations of the classical model. However, pure Celtic art survived on the periphery of the sprawling Roman empire, on the other side of the Channel. Ireland and what is now Great Britain would become the guardians of ancient Celtic forms evolved on the Continent over the previous five hundred years — Ireland because she had never been conquered by Rome, Britain because she was subdued at a later date and abandoned relatively early. During this era Celtic artefacts reached the

height of refinement, with ever more complex compass-drawn motifs adorning helmets, votive shields and the backing of mirrors.

After the 5th century AD, this **insular Celtic art** persisted for the most part in Ireland. Just as the Christian missionaries doubtless welcomed into their fold bards and filids – poets and seers, inheritors of Druidic wisdom – so Celtic motifs were put to work for the glorification of God. This was the age of the great illuminated books, the most famous of which, the Book of Kells, is considered to be one of the crowning glories of Irish and even European medieval art. The influence of the Irish school bore fruit across Europe in the wake of the Irish missionaries – from Wales, Northumbria and possibly Armorica (Ancient Brittany) to Switzerland and even northern Italy. The Viking invasions, around the year 1000, brought this chapter of art history to a savage conclusion.

Ancient Celtic culture has now disappeared into the mists of time. Yet here and there we still come across works of north-western European art inspired by Celtic models: unique pieces like Brian Boru's mysterious Irish harp with its ingenious decoration (13th century?) or knotwork patterns designed for Renaissance craftsmen by Leonardo da Vinci or Albrecht Dürer and others. It would seem that it was the popular arts that over the course of time best preserved the repertoire of simpler forms like the spiral, the triskele, the chainstitch and the knot. Nineteenth-century folklorists researched and took their inspiration from the art of Ireland, Wales, Scotland and Cornwall to imbue their work – embroidery, cabinet-making and ceramics – with a typically 'Atlantic feel'. In France it is of course Brittany that has inherited a taste for Celtic forms as a result of imported influences.

Should we then see in traditional Breton furniture, with its quatrefoils and sun and wheel motifs, a survival of a lost Celtic craft? And are the designs on the famous **Bigouden embroideries** one more revival of an age-old textile tradition? In reality, no answer can be found to these questions as there remain no written fragments or historical evidence – only hypotheses and artistic echoes. To poets and visionaries this heritage is fact; for others it is only the expression of a universal trend.

Study of the Seiz Breur movement of the 1930s, whose aim was to 'modernise' Breton craft tradition, sheds little light on the matter. However, their work did

Broderies d'un corsage bigouden du début du XXᵉ siècle. Collection musée de Bretagne, Rennes (détail)

Buffet de Jacques Philippe, 1938. Collection musée de Bretagne, Rennes. (détail)

produce a synthesis between the geometric formats of Art Deco and the motifs common to ancient Gaul, medieval Ireland and Breton folklore. The results, though promising, proved a mere flash in the pan due to the lack of funding and perhaps interest at the time, but they did leave a legacy for future designers. Indeed, in a post-war consumerist society overrun with mass production, craftsmen drew a certain inspiration, particularly in Brittany, from the work of the Seiz Breur: nowadays the auction rooms and the shelves of secondhand dealers are filled with sideboards, chairs and china with Breton-style geometric motifs, all somewhat trite and mass-produced.

From the 1970s Celtic art took off in a big way, especially in the fields of music and dance, jewellery and illustration. Indeed, against a background of anti-globalisation, there has been a more general movement amongst craftsmen to re-appropriate the symbols of the past in order to satisfy a passion for rediscovered vernacular cultures.

The aim of this book is to open a door into the world of the symbols and patterns that constitute Celtic art. It will introduce you to a wide spectrum of designs inspired by the diversity and mystery of Celtic history, as well as others reflecting my own particular interests. In some cases the designs have been deconstructed to clarify how they are formed.

This collection in no way claims to be exhaustive but hopefully will help you feel more at ease exploring other publications dealing with the Celtic world and its art forms. It may also encourage you to investigate other varieties of graphic art from different times and places.

Celtic illuminated manuscripts

From the 5th century AD Celtic art underwent a certain renaissance in Ireland and England. This was a period of transition: the Roman Empire had disintegrated and Celtic monasticism was growing in importance, notably in Ireland.

Celtic artists in Britain and Ireland were henceforth working for the glory of God and exporting their work and knowledge to the Continent. More specifically, the 7th, 8th and early 9th centuries are considered the golden age of Celtic art. Three masterpieces have come down to us from this era: the Book of Durrow, the Lindisfarne Gospels and the Book of Kells, and we will be constantly referring to these.

The Book of Durrow

In common with the two other works, the Book of Durrow is an evangeliary containing the gospels of Matthew, Mark, Luke and John.

Dating most probably from the mid-7th century, this gospel book offers us our earliest glimpse of high-quality Celtic ornamental work on vellum. In it ancient Celtic motifs mingle harmoniously with decorative elements derived from Roman, Byzantine, Pictish and Germanic sources.

The Book of Durrow is believed to have been started in Scotland and completed in southern Ireland, where Durrow Abbey is found. Today it is in the library of Trinity College, Dublin.

The Lindisfarne Gospels

Lindisfarne was a monastery founded on an island off the Northumbrian coast by Irish missionaries. This gospel book dates from the late 7th century and is famous for its sumptuous 'carpet pages', full-page illuminations featuring highly complex interlaced motifs. Because of the proximity of Lindisfarne to the Saxon kingdoms established in Northumbria during this time, the Gospels are generally seen as a synthesis of Germanic and Celtic elements. The book is now in the British Library in London.

The Book of Kells

This third evangeliary, dating from the early 9th century, is considered by some to be the masterpiece of the High Middle Ages in Europe. As early as the 1200s the historian Giraldus Cambrensis saw in it 'not the work of Man, but of Angels'. Like the other two gospel books, the Book of Kells contains full-page illuminations in the form of superbly crafted scenes from the life of Christ, such as the Virgin and Child, the betrayal by Judas, and the Temptation. The Monogram (or Chi-Rho) Page – so called from the first two letters of the Greek word for Christ – is one of the most dazzling examples of Celtic illumination. Like the Durrow Book, the Book of Kells is in the library of Trinity College, Dublin.

Some of the motifs featured in *Exploring and Creating Celtic Motifs* have been directly inspired by these sources; the rest are my own creations.

David Balade

Drawing materials

At the end of each chapter you will find diagrams explaining the construction of motifs discussed in the text. To make the designs you will need the following items, all readily obtainable from stationery or artists' suppliers.

For drawing:
- an HB pencil or mechanical pencil
- a soft rubber
- black felt-tips (indelible ink and fine points), or architect's pens for use with Indian ink
- a flat, graduated ruler
- a pair of compasses
- sufficiently thick paper such as Bristol or 180 g vellum.

For colouring:
- watercolour felt-tip pens
- gouache brushes, no. 2 for the finest detail.

The Boatmen's Pillar: the 'Jupiter' stone, face D (bull with three cranes).

The three cranes recall the sacred nature of the number three, a theme recurrent in Celtic tradition and inherited by this sculpture of the Gallo-Roman period.

Spirals

The spiral is probably one of the first abstract motifs constructed by man. Swirling visions of water, air and fire doubtless held particular attraction for Celtic artists who recognised in them the most vivid expression of the energy of an ever-changing universe.

The spiral is a hypnotic, fascinating image. Its form seems at one moment to draw us into the centre of existence itself and the next to fling us out towards another world.

Constructing a motif Spiral 1

Foliate motif inspired by spirals from the most famous carpet page of the Book of Durrow, folio 3 v°. On this page, the spirals take leaf-like forms. The overall design evokes a profusion of plant life, a leitmotif found throughout Celtic decorative art, on brooches, the backs of mirrors, helmets, and so on. This exuberant representation of organic forms is often suggestive of Art Nouveau.

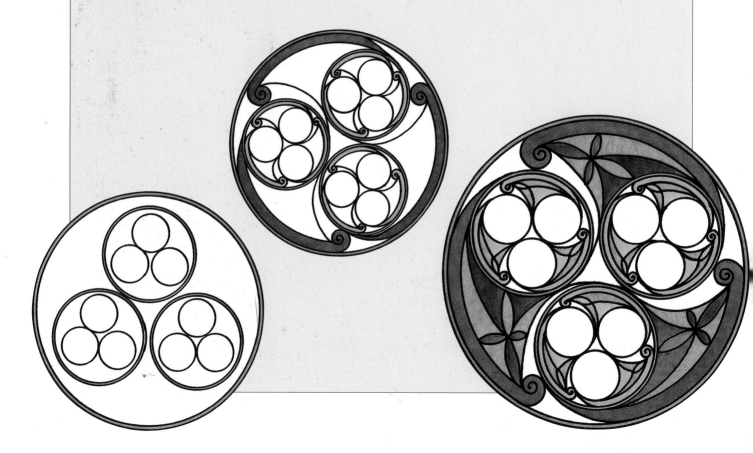

Experimenting with colour

Spiral 1

These examples are inspired by a double spiral in the Lindisfarne Gospels. Celtic art exploited the possibilities of compass-drawn designs to the limit, with not only single but double and triple versions, i.e. with two or three lines originating from a central point. Gold and silver objects from the 4th century BC — and carved bones presumably used as a drafting surface to sketch motifs on — reveal evidence of the use of compass points. The double spirals on these two pages recall the Taoist motif of Yin and Yang.

Experimenting with form

Spiral 1

Spirals based on those of folio 33 r° of the Book of Kells: cross with eight medallions.
The largest (facing page) is the closest to the original.
The spirals from this folio are incredibly complex considering their actual dimensions; presumably Celtic artists must already have been using magnifying-glasses in their scriptoria (workshops) to attain such a level of precision.

Constructing a motif Spiral 2

Tetraskel (fire symbol). Breton motif derived from the region's traditional hevoud, adapted for a sideboard by Joseph Savina, 1938. The hevoud – a four-armed spiral cross – is a development of the triskele (three arms) and is purported to bring good luck.

Experimenting with colour

Spiral 2

This spiral was inspired by an example from the Book of Durrow. Here we see triple spirals; the threefold repetition of certain elements of the motif inevitably suggests the triskele, a quintessentially Celtic motif, adopted notably by the Bretons of Armorica.

Experimenting with form

Spiral 2

Whirlpools

Original design, based on spirals from the Book of Durrow.

The multiple interlocking triskeles are inspired by carvings on the Aberlemno Cross, Scotland.

Original design. The triskele unravels into scrolls echoing the sinuous forms of Art Nouveau.

Original creation, inspired by 1930s designs combining Celtic and Art Deco motifs in the style of the Seiz Breur movement.

How to draw ...

Three equidistant circles within a larger circle

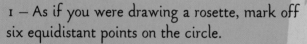

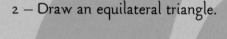

1 — As if you were drawing a rosette, mark off six equidistant points on the circle.

2 — Draw an equilateral triangle.

3 — The centres for the smaller circles (see 4) are where the medians — the dotted lines connecting the centre of the circle to an apex of the triangle — intersect with the sides of the triangle.

4 — To prevent the smaller circles intersecting, keep their radii within the medians.

A simple spiral

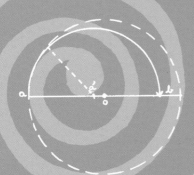

1 — On the diameter of the circle select an arbitrary point a'. Draw first a semicircle of radius aa'. This gives point b.

2 — Now draw the semicircle with centre O and radius Ob. This gives point b'.

3 — Next draw the semicircle of radius a'b'. This gives b".

4 — Repeat with further semicircles, using centres O and a' alternately.

How to draw ...

Double spiral

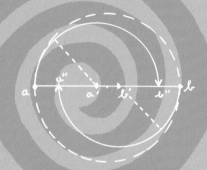

1 – On the diameter ab of the circle, with the aid of compasses, mark the points a' and b', equidistant from the centre.

2 – Draw two semicircles: with centre a' and radius aa', to obtain point b"; with centre b' and radius bb' to obtain point a".

3 – Now draw in the semicircle with centre a' and radius a'a", giving b'''. Continue in the same way; this variation on the simple spiral depends on the alternation of semicircles with centres a' and b'.

Triple spiral

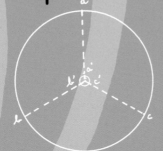

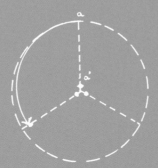

1 — Referring to page 24, determine points a, b and c, equidistant on the circle. Draw three radii linking the centre of the circle to these points. Now draw a second, small circle with the same centre. At the intersections of the small circle with the three radii, mark points a', b' and c', also equidistant.

2 — Starting from a, draw a semicircle with centre a' and radius aa'. This gives a point where the arc and the next median intersect.

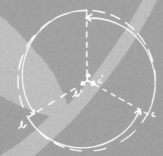

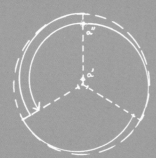

3 — Repeat the operation for arcs with centres b' and c' and with radii bb' and cc' respectively.

4 — At the intersection of aa' and the arc starting from c, mark a". Now draw an arc starting from a" with centre a' and radius a'a". Repeat the process for the remaining two arcs.

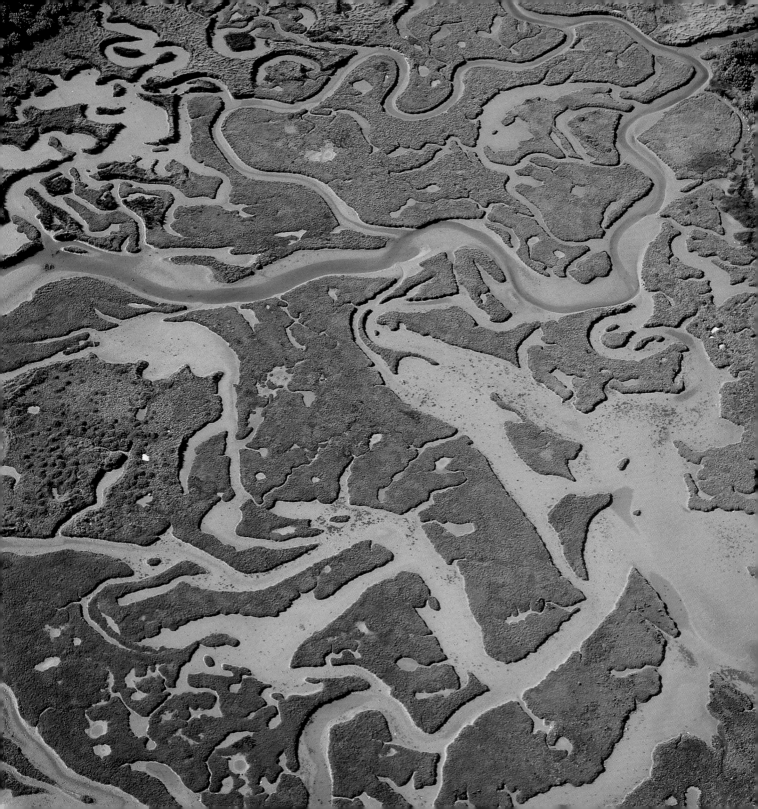

Knots

Along with the spiral, knots are one of the most recognisable features of Celtic art through the centuries. These motifs, used in profusion, often decorating every available surface, were probably inspired by the reticulated filigree work of the Teutonic goldsmiths, a technique absorbed by the Celts at the start of the Middle Ages. Besides suggesting an instinctive dislike of empty space, the knots, which are a marked characteristic of these art forms, probably symbolise immortal life, endless like the ribbon from which they are formed.

Constructing a motif Knot 1

Motif inspired by a decorated medallion from St John's Gospel, Book of Durrow, folio 129 v°. The design resembles that found on certain Irish brooches of the High Middle Ages. Irish goldsmiths acquired an undisputed mastery of the techniques of filigree, granulation and enamelling and it was most likely from them that artists of the local scriptoria took their inspiration.

Experimenting with colour

Knot 1

Knotwork frieze from the page featuring St Mark's lion, Book of Durrow, folio 191 v°. Notice how this example consists of several ribbons rather than a single one as is more usual.

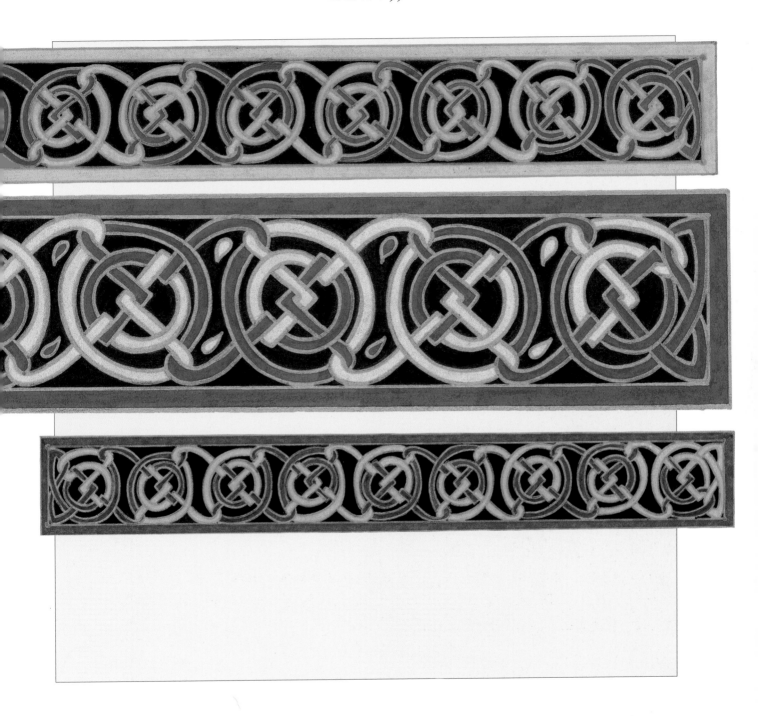

Experimenting with form

Knot 1

The carved stones of northern England, Scotland and Wales are difficult to date precisely and are among the most enigmatic examples of Celtic art. Perhaps boundary markers or indicating sacred sites, they reveal the amazing precision and attention to detail of contemporary stonemasons.

This page: Sculpted motif on the Nigg Stone, Ross and Cromarty, Scotland.

Opposite: Sculpted motif on the Collieburn Stone (Sutherland) and Glamis Stone (Angus), Scotland.

Constructing a motif Knot 2

Motifs from Auguste Racinet's *L'Ornement polychrome* (1885) combined to resemble the carpet pages of Irish manuscripts. From the early 1800s the distinction began to be made between the iconography of the Celts and that of the rest of medieval art. Racinet's sourcebook appeared at a time when Scottish and Irish artists were rediscovering their Celtic legacy in the wake of various political movements.

Experimenting with colour

Knot 2

Friezes consisting of interlacing palmettes inspired by the ornamentation on a Renaissance chest (Rennes Museum). These palmettes, reminiscent of Bigouden embroidery peacock-tail motifs, demonstrate a certain continuity in the iconography of the decorative arts in Brittany.

Interlacing ribbons inspired by carving on a Gothic Renaissance chest of 1630 (Quimper Museum).

Experimenting with form

Knot 2

For a long time Breton cabinet-makers perpetuated decorative elements from the past to satisfy local tastes and habits. This may partly explain the seemingly incongruent use of the term 'Gothic Renaissance style' for a much later historical period.

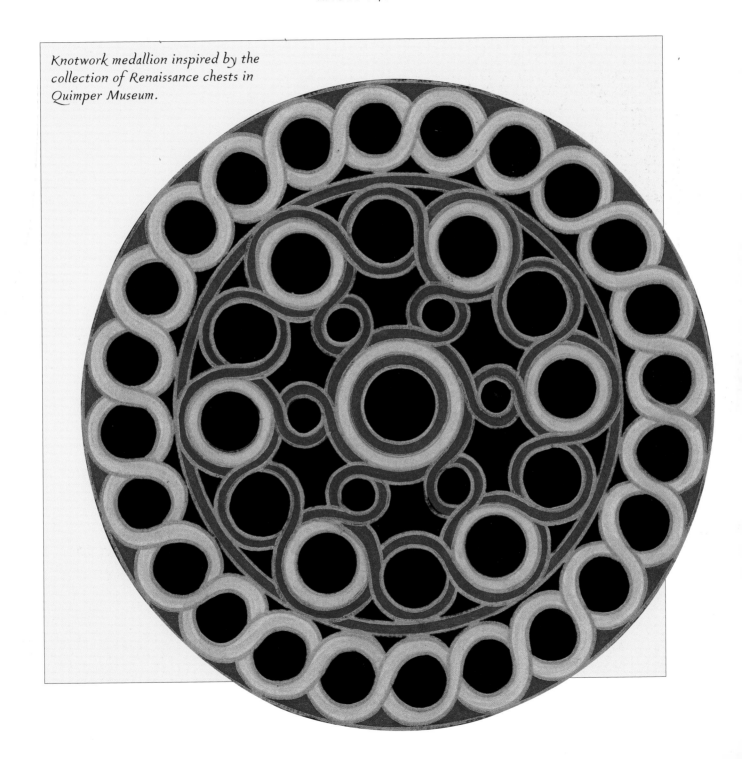

Knotwork medallion inspired by the collection of Renaissance chests in Quimper Museum.

How to draw ...

Solomon's knot

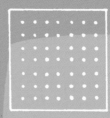

1 — Draw a square of eight units per side and divide it into a grid. Place a dot at the intersections of the verticals and horizontals.

2 — Link the points as shown, ignoring the interlacing for the moment.

3 — Following the lines produced in this way, add ribbons as shown in the diagram with the aid of the intersection points.

4 — Fill in the enclosed spaces and complete the knotwork, remembering the rule 'over, under'.

The Meigle knot

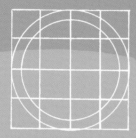

1 — Draw a square of four units per side. Starting from its centre draw two concentric circles. Divide the big square into a grid.

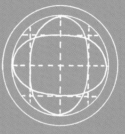

2 — With the aid of the grid draw the first lines of the knot design freehand.

3 — Following these lines, draw the ribbons freehand; ignore the 'over, under' rule for the moment.

4 — Fill in the enclosed spaces and complete the knotwork using the 'over, under' rule.

How to draw ...

Frieze with palmettes page 38

1 – Draw a horizontal axis, then draw arcs touching the axis at their further points and with their centres on it. From the same centres draw smaller arcs so as to create ribbon-like bands.

2 – As on page 25 (simple spiral), add spirals starting from the end points of these arcs.

3 – Draw a horizontal band parallel to the axis, linking it to the spirals. Place small circles on the sides of the wider arcs; their centre is the intersection of the axis and the arcs, the radius being the width of the band.

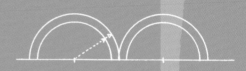

4 – Complete the knot design using the 'over, under' rule.

Knotwork frieze

1 — Draw a horizontal axis and two circles of equal radius centred on this axis. With the aid of compasses and a pencil, reproduce the distance between these two centres along the axis as in the diagram.

2 — Draw two other circles starting from the points determined with the compasses. Add diagonals joining the centres of the circles and their intersection points. Finally, just above and below the intersections, draw lines parallel to the horizontal axis.

3 — Create ribbons with the help of the lines drawn in (2), either with a ruler and compasses or freehand.

4 — Complete the knotwork using the 'over, under' rule.

Flora and fauna

In Celtic legend, men and gods could change their shapes to become animals, plants and even rocks or stones. These shape-shiftings at will were also a means to escape from reality. Celtic art — art of the imagination — is an interpretation of this constantly changing fantasy world, using natural forms to create illusion: forms blend into one another, limbs metamorphose into branches, eyes into leaves or the heads of fabulous beasts.

Constructing a motif
Flora and fauna 1

Inspired by the gold-embossed bronze disk found at Auvers-sur-Oise in the île de France and dating from the 4th century BC, this design clearly illustrates the freedom employed by Celtic artists in the treatment of certain motifs of Mediterranean or even Oriental origin. Here two dragons facing each other around a tree of life become a pattern of lyres and lotuses. The overall effect, through its symmetry, is of some curious flower.

Experimenting with colour

Flora and fauna 1

Personal creations inspired by the peacock-tail motifs of traditional Bigouden embroidery. The peacock tail — a stylised form of classical palmette according to some sources — elegantly symbolises the confusion between the animal and plant worlds, so characteristic of Irish and Welsh folk tales.

Experimenting with form

Flora and fauna 1

Interlaced birds inspired by the Lindisfarne Gospels. Birds, in particular bird heads, were among the favourite animal motifs of Celtic artists because of the ease with which they could be transformed, as they had been since classical antiquity, into organic scrolls on a wide variety of metal artefacts. In the Middle Ages, it was chiefly the graceful bodies that fascinated artists and led to these complex interlacings.

Interlaced dogs, from the Lindisfarne Gospels. Teutonic peoples were particularly fond of dog motifs, including the Angles and Saxons who colonised Britain around the 4th century AD. These dogs often resembled the dragon figures on the prows of the Viking drakkar (longship). Continual exchanges between Ireland, Scotland and England at the time would explain the motif's adoption by the Celts.

Constructing a motif Flora and fauna 2

Tree of life and interlaced birds from the Book of Kells, folio 2 r°. The tree
of life is one of the most common motifs in Celtic illuminated manuscripts.
Doubtless inspired by the ancient Mesopotamian tree of life, the motif
appears to have passed into Christian iconography via the Byzantines to
become the Tree of Jesse. Whatever its origin, Celtic artists, with their
passion for plant forms and interlacing, readily integrated it into their
pictorial vocabulary.

Experimenting with colour

Flora and fauna 2

Two dogs and birds from the Lindisfarne Gospels. The dogs symbolise the earth, the birds the air: a metaphor of the communion between body and spirit.

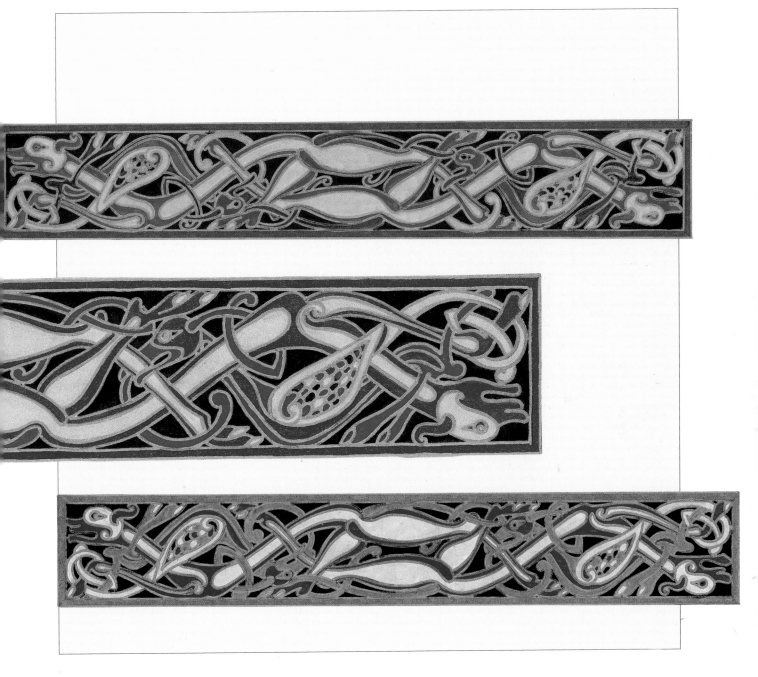

Two interlaced dogs forming a lemniscate, surrounded by the tree of life: motifs inspired by a panel in Christ Church Cathedral, Dublin. In Indian tradition, the lemniscate — an endless ribbon in figure-of-eight form — symbolises the concept of universal harmony and the infinite cycle of existence.

Experimenting with colour

Flora and fauna 2

Two birds in symmetrical pose, inspired by the Book of Kells, folio 124 r°. These are probably eagles, symbols of St John. As well as St John, the Book of Kells, the Durrow Book and the Lindisfarne Gospels feature traditional emblems of St Mark (winged lion), St Luke (ox) and St Matthew (angel).

Bestiary

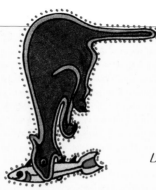

Lion of St Mark (Lindisfarne Gospels, folio 93 v°).

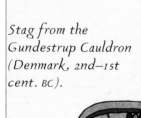

Peacock (Book of Kells, folio 309 r°).

Otter with salmon (Book of Kells, folio 34 r°, Monogram Page).

Moth (Book of Kells, folio 34 r°, Monogram Page).

Serpent (Pictish carved stone, 5th–4th cent. BC, Scotland).

Cats and mice fighting over a host (Book of Kells, folio 34 r°, Monogram Page).

Stag from the Gundestrup Cauldron (Denmark, 2nd–1st cent. BC).

Hare and hound (Book of Kells, folio 48 r°).

Eagle of St John (Book of Armagh, 8th–9th cent. AD, Ireland).

How to draw ...
The Bigouden peacock motif

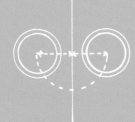

1 — Draw an axis and two equidistant circles.

2 — Draw a first series of arcs starting from point a; point b (the intersection of the axis and the smallest arc) will be the centre of the second series of arcs.

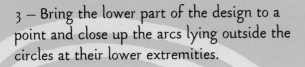

3 — Bring the lower part of the design to a point and close up the arcs lying outside the circles at their lower extremities.

4 — Add decorative elements as illustrated.

How to draw ...

Interlaced dogs page 53

1 — With the aid of vertical and horizontal axes, draw the basic silhouettes of the two dogs.

2 — Put in the other lines, paying special attention to the intersections. Use dotted lines at this stage for the ears and tails.

3 — Fill in remaining details, again taking care over the intersections and observing the 'over, under' rule.

Two interlaced birds
(from the Book of Kells)

1 — With the aid of a vertical axis draw the silhouettes of the two birds.

2 — Add the body lines, paying special attention to the intersections and using dotted lines at this stage for the 'ears'.

3 — Add remaining details; again take care with the intersections and remember the 'over, under' rule for the interlacing.

Mazes

From the Bronze Age to Ireland of the Middle Ages, the maze motif with its innumerable twists and turns crops up in settings as diverse as the megaliths of prehistoric tumuli to the folios of exquisitely crafted Bibles. Some believe the maze to be a kind of spiral modified by a desire for right angles. For others, this mysterious symbol represents the unpredictable windings of earthly life ... the path of an endless quest.

Constructing a motif Maze 1

Carpet page inspired by motifs from the Book of Kells and the Lindisfarne Gospels. In Celtic illuminated books, carpet pages are those covered entirely with motifs. The patterns are often so complex as to suggest a connection with lost masterpieces of textile art. It is possible that exchanges of artefacts between royal courts and Celtic monasteries may have led to Oriental carpets reaching Ireland – thus providing inspiration for certain local artists.

Experimenting with colour

Maze 1

Central motif from the Lindisfarne Gospels. In illuminated manuscripts mazes most frequently serve as borders to frame a figure of Christ. They were also placed in the corners of knotwork borders to relieve the monotony of the decoration. Here, as throughout the chapter, the maze has been isolated and treated as a subject in its own right.

Experimenting with form

Maze 1

This page: Central motif from the Book of Kells with border adapted from an example in the Lindisfarne Gospels.

Opposite page: Central medallion from the Book of Kells. While the maze motif is common to many cultures, this systematically diagonal treatment is uniquely Celtic.

Experimenting with colour

Maze 2

Central motif from the Book of Kells. It looks strangely modern, a little like a microprocessor circuit.

Variation of form Maze 2

In Celtic illustrated manuscripts we also come across the traditional, circular form of maze as illustrated on these two pages. In ancient times, this design was used on Minoan coinage – perhaps suggesting the labyrinth Daedalus built to hold the Minotaur – and in curious rock carvings in the Camonica Valley, Italy. A similar pattern is found in the mysterious pavement maze in the nave of Chartres cathedral.

Opposite page: Central medallion from the Mac Durnan Gospels.

This page: Central medallion from the Book of Kells.

How to draw ...

Maze from the Book of Kells

1 — Draw a square of six units per side and divide it diagonally into a grid as in the diagram; this grid forms the basis of the design. Now fill in the first diagonals of the pattern.

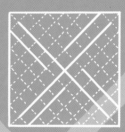

2 — Add the lines branching at right angles as illustrated.

3 — Finally add the lines parallel to the sides to complete the borders, and fill in the resulting triangles.

Simple maze frieze from the Book of Kells

1 — Draw a band three units wide with a grid as in the previous example. Fill in the first equidistant diagonals and add short right-angled branches.

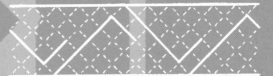

2 — Draw the lines parallel to the sides of the band, starting from the angles in (1). These lines terminate in acute angles.

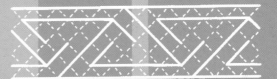

3 — As shown, fill in two small isosceles triangles of equal size, using as bases the parallel lines drawn in (2).

How to draw ...

Complex variation of maze on page 77

1 — Draw a band 4.5 units wide and 16 long with grid as shown. Fill in the first diagonal lines, which end in right angles.

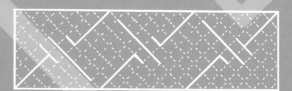

2 — Draw the lines parallel to the sides of the band.

3 — Fill in the triangles.

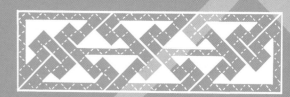

Maze from the Book of Kells

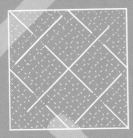

1 — Form a gridded square with sides of ten units. Draw in the first diagonals.

2 — Add the branches; use the centre point as your axis of symmetry.

3 — Draw a border a half-unit wide linking the angles thus formed. Fill in the enclosed spaces and finish off the spirals with small right angles.

A Celtic alphabet

The Celtic world fully discovered the art of book illustration with the arrival of the first Christian missionaries at the dawn of the Middle Ages. A cultural fusion took place between two civilisations, one centred upon the written word, the other living through its imagination, resulting in masterpieces such as the Book of Kells, the Durrow Book and the Lindisfarne Gospels. In a spirit rooted in ancient Celtic art, letters assumed the forms of plants and animals — Irish inventions that would eventually influence the technique of illumination throughout medieval Europe.

Capital A: Inspired by the
Book of Kells

A: Original creation

B: Original creation

C: Original creation

D: Inspired by the Book of Kells

E: *Inspired by the Book of Kells*
F: *Inspired by the Book of Kells*
G: *Original creation*
Capital H: *Original creation*
H: *Inspired by the Book of Kells*

I: *Original creation*

Capital J: *Original creation*

J: *Original creation*

K: *Inspired by the Book of Kells*

L: *Inspired by the Book of Kells*

M: Inspired by the Cathach psalter attrib. to St Columba, c. AD 600

N: Inspired by the Lindisfarne Gospels

O: Inspired by the Lindisfarne Gospels

Capital O: Inspired by the Lindisfarne Gospels; the area surrounding the central medallion has been left blank for a less cluttered effect.

P: Original creation

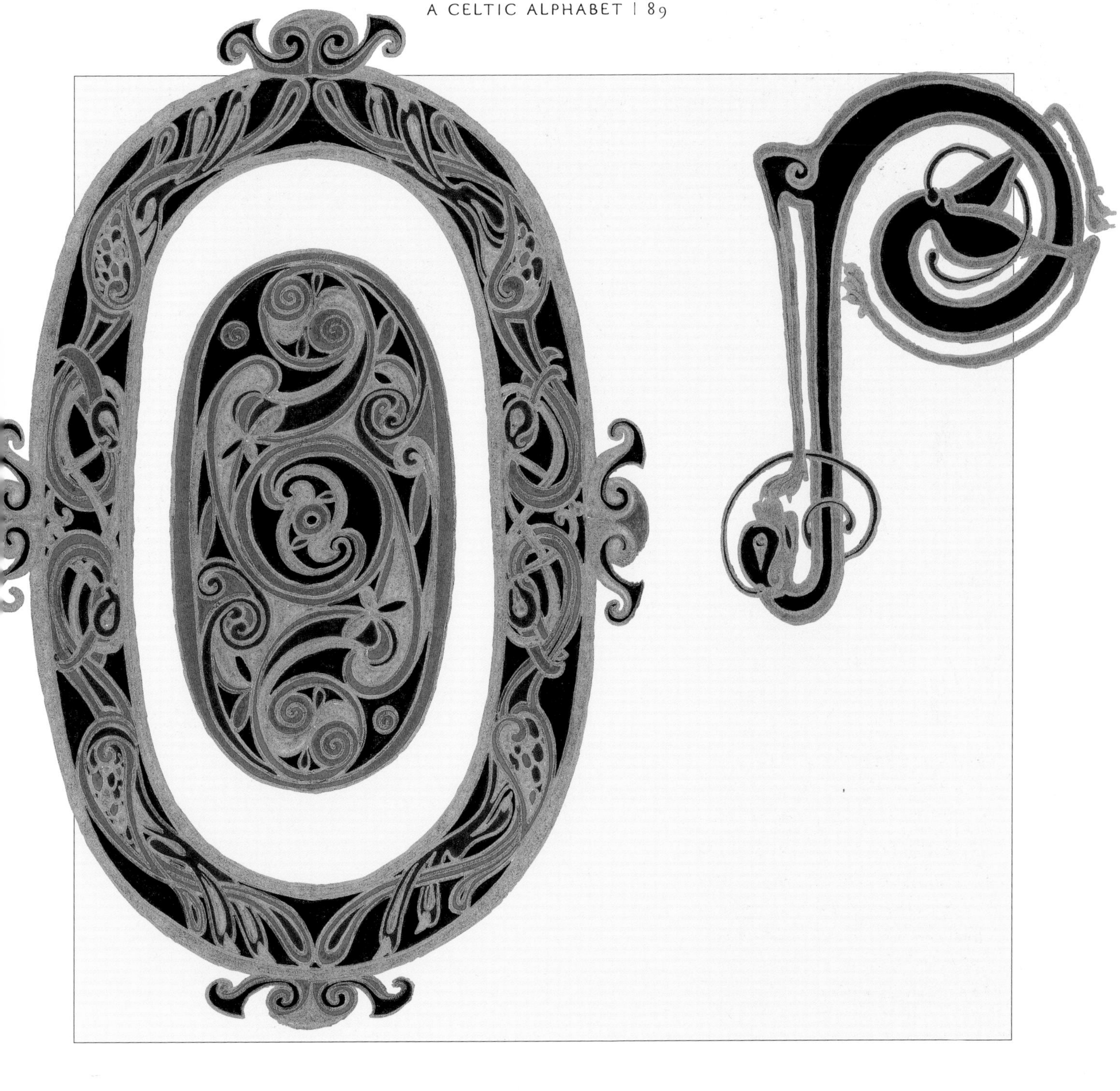

Q: Inspired by the Durham Cassiodorus
R: Adapted from the Book of Kells
Capital R: Inspired by the Book of Kells
S: Original creation

T: Inspired by the Book of Kells
U: Original creation
V: Original creation
W: Original creation

X: Inspired by the Monogram Page in the
Book of Kells

Y: Original creation

Z: Z-rod, after symbol common on Pictish
carved stones

Spirals

*After the Lagore Buckle,
County Meath, Ireland,
c. AD 800.*

*Spiral inspired by a
detail from folio 33 r of
the Book of Kells, early
9th century.*

Triskele: author's original design.

Knotwork
pre-12th century

*Knot from the Britford Stone,
nr. Salisbury, England.*

*Knot from the Ulbster Stone,
Caithness, Scotland.*

Knots from the St Madoes Stone, Perthshire, Scotland.

Flora and fauna

a bestiary

*Interlaced birds,
Book of Kells,
early 9th century.*

*Interlaced birds,
Book of Kells,
early 9th century,
folio 32 v.*

*Interlaced dragons,
Book of Kells, early 9th
century, folio 29 r.*

Mazes
pre-12th century

Maze, adapted from the Nigg Cross, Ross and Cromarty, Scotland.

Maze from the Book of Kells, early 9th century.

*Maze inspired by the
Lindisfarne Gospels,
late 7th century.*